SERIES TITLES

TURN OF THE CENTURY AND THE GREAT WAR
was produced by McRae Books Srl
Borgo S. Croce, 8 – 50122 – Florence (Italy)
info@mcraebooks.com
www.mcraebooks.com

Publishers: Anne McRae, Marco Nardi
Art Director: Marco Nardi
Series Editor: Anne McRae
Author: Neil Morris
Layouts: Nick Leggett, Starry Dog Books Ltd
Title Editor: Vicky Egan
Project Editor: Loredana Agosta
Research: Vicky Egan
Repro: Litocolor, Florence

Main Illustrations: MM Comunicazione
(Manuela Cappon, Monica Favilli, Gianni Sbragi,
Cecilia Scutti) pp. 20-21, 26-27, 37; Lorenzo Cecchi:
3, 8-9, 4-35
Other illustrations: Lorenzo Cecchi, Michela
Gaudenzi, MM Comunicazione (Manuela Cappon,
Monica Favilli, Gianni Sbragi, Cecilia Scutti), Paola
Ravaglia, Studio Stalio (Alessandro Cantucci, Fabiano
Fabbrucci, Margherita Salvadori)
Maps: Paola Baldanzi
Photography: THE BRIDGEMAN ART LIBRARY: 6tr,
6cl, 7tr, 7cr, 9cl, 10c, 14tl, 14tr, 14 cl, 15b, 18-19b,
19tl, 21tr, 24cl, 27cl, 28cr, 28tr, 29cr, 30-31c, 34br,
36tl, 37tl, 38br, 39bl, 40cl, 42-43b, 43l, 45l; @
Caroline Townsend by SIAE 2009/Beatrice Webb
House, Dorking, Surrey, UK 19cd; @ Canadian War
Museum, Ottawa, Canada/ The Bridgeman Art Library
38cd e 41; @ John Strickland Goodall by SIAE 2009 /
Christopher Wood Gallery, London, UK 16-17b; @
Frederick William Elwell by SIAE 2009 / Ferens Art
Gallery, Hull City Museums e Art Galleries 17cl; @
Imperial War Museum, London, UK / The Bridgeman
Art Library 32-33c; @Look and Learn/ The Bridgeman
Art Library / Private Collection 6-7b: @ Marc Chagall
by SIAE 2009 44cl; John Galt by SIAE / Museum of
London, UK 16ar; @ Pablo Picasso by SIAE 2009
44ar. GETTY IMAGES: 12b, 12br. THE ART
ARCHIVE: 6bl, The Art Archive/ Culver Pictures 8tr,
The Art Archive / Eileen Tweedy 36cr, The Art Archive
/ Imperial War Museum 28cl, The Art Archive /
Private Collection / Marc Charmet 43bl, The Art
Archive / Private Collection London 30cl ; @ The Art
Archive / Ocean Memorabilia Collection: 23cr, 23cl,
23br, 22tr, 22tl. THE KOBAL COLLECTION: Edison /
The Kobal Collection 11tl/ Epoch/The Kobal
Collection 11r, Keystone/The Kobal Collection 11b,
Mèliès/The Kobal Collection 10bl; @ Yanco/Tao/
Recorded Picture Co/ The Kobal Collection 25b; @
20th Century Fox/Paramount/The Kobal Collection/
Wallace Merie W.:22-23b e 23tl. All other images:
McRae Books archive.

Consultant: Professor Hew Strachan, MA, PhD, FRSE,
FRHistS, Hon D. Univ (Paisley), Chichele Professor of
the History of War, All Souls College, Oxford
University, UK.

The Turn of the Century and the Great War
 ISBN 9788860981820

2009923564

Printed and bound in Malaysia.

HISTORY

Turn of the Century
and the Great War

Neil Morris

Consultant: Professor Hew Strachan
Chichele Professor of the History of War, All Souls College, Oxford, UK

Zak
BOOKS

Contents

Around 1912 dresses became more slender.

TIMELINE

	1900	1905	1910	1912
UNITED STATES OF AMERICA	Presidency of Theodore Roosevelt, 1901–09.	American civil rights leader Susan B. Anthony dies, 1906. Roosevelt wins Nobel Peace prize for negotiating end of Russo-Japanese war.	Anti-monopoly laws are introduced in 1911, breaking up the powerful Standard Oil Company.	
GREAT BRITAIN		Informal Triple Entente is made between France, Britain, and Russia, 1907. Reign of Edward VII, 1901–10.		Edwardian costume reflects growing emancipation for women. Corsets are on the way out.
INDIA, CHINA, AND JAPAN	An international force crushes the Boxer rebels in China, 1901.	The All-India Muslim League is founded in 1906 to protect Muslim rights.	King George V is crowned Emperor of India at the Delhi Durbar, 1911.	
THE OTTOMAN EMPIRE AND CENTRAL EUROPE	Already in decline, the Ottoman Empire controls only Asia Minor (the Anatolia region of present-day Turkey) and parts of the Balkans and the Middle East.			
RUSSIA		The Bloody Sunday massacre of unarmed workers takes place in St. Petersburg.		
THE GREAT WAR		The major European powers are steadily building up their military power.	A Great Naval Review at Spithead (in the English Channel) shows off the powerful British fleet, 1909.	
ARTS, SCIENCE, PIONEERS	Orville and Wilbur Wright make the world's first successful powered flight in their plane *Flyer*.		Henry Ford launches his Model-T automobile in 1908, and sells more than 10,000 in a year.	

Introduction

There were great technological achievements at the beginning of the 20th century. They included the first powered flight, by the Wright brothers, in 1903. Five years later another American, Henry Ford, launched his popular Model-T motor car. In other parts of the world, the early 20th century was a time of great social change. There were revolutions in Russia and China. Old empires that had been successful for centuries—such as that of the Ottomans—were in decline. In Europe, there was a build-up of military power among many nations. Alliances were cemented and political tension mounted, until war finally broke out in 1914. This book tells the story of the pre-war period and describes the causes and horrors of the First World War (1914–18). It also covers developments in science and the arts, discovery and exploration, as well as the struggles and achievements of the growing women's movement.

Wilhelm II (1859–1941) was the eldest son of Frederick III and Princess Victoria, daughter of Queen Victoria of England.

Field telephones like this one were used for communication, and there were a small number of wireless sets.

1914

Film studios are established in the Hollywood district of Los Angeles.

Suffragettes march on Washington, D.C.

Irish Home Rule Act provides for a separate Parliament in Ireland.

War is triggered by the assassination of Franz Ferdinand, heir to the Austro-Hungarian throne.

Russia joins the Allies in the First World War as part of the Triple Entente with Britain and France.

Germany declares war on Russia and then France.

German troops invade Belgium. Britain declares war on Germany.

1915

A direct wireless service is established between the US and Japan.

The British government appeals for women to join a Register of Women for War Service.

The first Zeppelin raids are made on London.

Japan presents China with an ultimatum: Twenty-One Demands. These include the demand that China agrees to Japanese control over Manchuria.

The British steamship Lusitania is sunk without warning off the coast of Ireland by a German submarine. 1,198 people drown.

1916

Woodrow Wilson is re-elected President by a narrow margin.

The Ottoman Turks fight a guerrilla war with the Arabs, who are helped by British army officer T. E. Lawrence (1888–1935).

1917

Conscription is introduced in the US.

General Sir Edmund Allenby (British commander of the Palestine Front) captures Jerusalem from the Ottomans.

The Russian Revolution.

The United States declares war on Germany.

The Third Battle of Ypres (also known as Passchendaele) is fought in Belgium..

1918

President Wilson's proposals for future peace, the "Fourteen Points," are delivered to Congress.

The 'flu epidemic spreads.

November 11, the Great War officially ends.

Grain riots in southern India, and 'flu kills hundreds of thousands of people.

The Early 20th Century

The nations of Europe faced major upheavals during the period 1900 to 1918. Before the war, there were social changes in some countries, but reforms were held up by the events of 1914. In Ireland, for example, the introduction of home rule was suspended, leading to rebellion. For four years, the First World War, also called the Great War, dominated people's lives, as millions of men were sent off to fight.

The ball was a fashionable event among the members of high society in the 1900s. This painting shows a gala evening in Vienna, the capital of Austria-Hungary.

In 1904, King Edward VII visited the Austro-Hungarian spa town of Marienbad (Marianske Lazne in the present-day Czech Republic).

La Belle Époque

In France, the years before the First World War became known as the Belle Époque ("beautiful period"). For middle- and upper-class people, it was a time of social elegance and cultural refinement. For the wealthy, life was settled and comfortable, and there was a growing freedom for artists and intellectuals. However, there was hardship among working-class families, many of whom turned to labor movements to better their situation. As war approached, many socialists believed that working men would never fight each other, but for most people national interests overcame class differences.

The Shadow of War

Early in the century, many European nations were politically stable. An exception was Portugal, where revolutionaries overthrew the king and formed a republic. But France and Britain felt threatened by Germany's growing power, Austria-Hungary was in disagreement with Serbia, and Russia was worried about its borders around the Black Sea. Conflicts and tensions led to the increased importance of political alliances.

End of Empires

Two major empires—the Russian and Ottoman—declined during the first decade of the century. The first revolution struck Russia in 1905 (see page 42), and in the final year of the Great War the last Romanov tsar was murdered. Ottoman decline (see pages 26–27) led to military defeats and the end of the empire after the Great War. The defeated Dual Monarchy of Austria-Hungary was also replaced by separate republics.

The Russian royal family, photographed in 1914. They were all killed four years later.

The Cost of the War

Out of more than 65 million men sent to war, some 10 million were killed and 21 million were wounded. Millions more were severely damaged by the horrors they witnessed. Women and children at home suffered great hardship (see pages 36–37). Some men wrote about their experiences, including the so-called war poets. One of the most famous was Wilfred Owen, who was given a military award but was killed in action just a week before the end of the war.

The Military Cross was awarded to British army officers for "gallantry during active operations against the enemy."

Women's rights campaigner Christabel Pankhurst (see page 18) incites the crowds in Trafalgar Square, London.

A New Kind of War

When war came, the political leaders of the nations involved assured their people that it would be over quickly. But the battle plans of both sides proved to be optimistic and sometimes unworkable, leading to stalemate. The situation was not helped by the use of new weapons, such as machine guns, tanks, airplanes, and poison gas. On the Western Front, deadlocked trench warfare dragged on, with huge numbers of lives being sacrificed to gain a few miles of churned-up land.

The new weapons of the Great War changed the way that wars would be fought in the future.

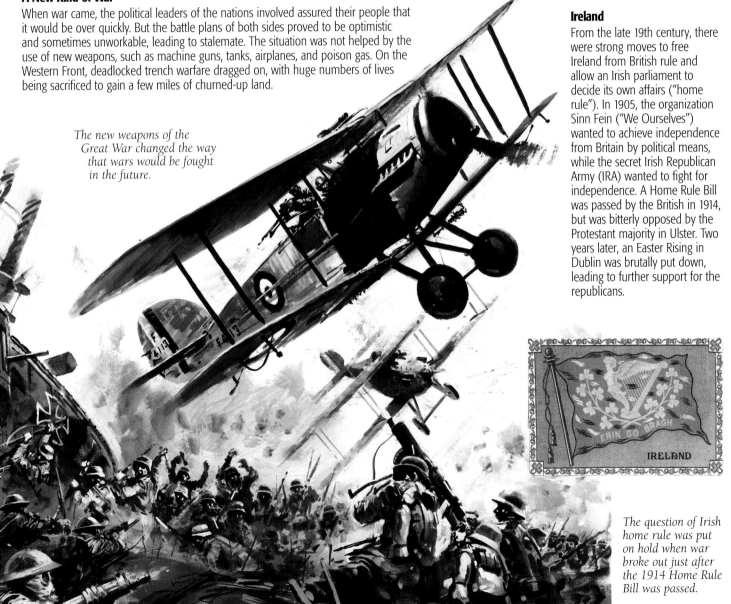

Ireland

From the late 19th century, there were strong moves to free Ireland from British rule and allow an Irish parliament to decide its own affairs ("home rule"). In 1905, the organization Sinn Fein ("We Ourselves") wanted to achieve independence from Britain by political means, while the secret Irish Republican Army (IRA) wanted to fight for independence. A Home Rule Bill was passed by the British in 1914, but was bitterly opposed by the Protestant majority in Ulster. Two years later, an Easter Rising in Dublin was brutally put down, leading to further support for the republicans.

The question of Irish home rule was put on hold when war broke out just after the 1914 Home Rule Bill was passed.

The Wright brothers' Flyer had a small petrol engine. Its first flight, on 17 December 1903, lasted just 12 seconds. The final flight of the day lasted 59 seconds and covered 853 feet (260 m).

First Flights

In 1903, bicycle-makers Orville and Wilbur Wright made the world's first successful powered flights, at Kitty Hawk, North Carolina. They used a method of twisting the wings to control their early aircraft. In the following years, aviation developed quickly. By 1911, the American inventor Glenn Curtiss (1878–1930) was building the first planes for the US Navy, having shown that they could take off and land on ships.

Child Labor

The development of the US textile industry had depended heavily on child labor, as it had done in Britain and other European countries. There was little regulation, and such laws as existed varied throughout the states. This meant that unscrupulous factory-owners could exploit young workers, whose parents needed their income. The first federal law restricting child labor was not brought in until 1916.

Children working at a Carolina cotton mill in 1908.

The USA at the Turn of the Century

In the United States there was a continuing rise in industry and big business during the early years of the 20th century. Motor cars were mass-produced, and the age of aviation began. These developments had a great influence on American society in general, as more people moved from the countryside to the growing cities. By 1916, almost half of the population of 100 million people lived in urban areas.

An early Curtiss biplane. Some useful developments were a wheeled undercarriage and an upright sitting position for the pilot.

Chinese Exclusion Act

A temporary Chinese Exclusion Act had become law in 1882. It was renewed ten years later and, in 1902, the Act was made indefinite. This was the first US immigration law aimed at a particular ethnic group. It was caused by concern in the western states at the large number of Chinese workers on the expanding railroads. Like many others, Chinese immigrants had also been tempted by the California gold rush.

Many immigrant families kept up their own traditions. These Chinese parents are celebrating their son's birthday.

Above: the killing of the president of USA, William McKinley.

About 28,000 buildings were destroyed by the San Francisco earthquake and fire. Burst water pipes hampered attempts to put the fires out.

The San Francisco Earthquake

Early on the morning of 18 April 1906, the city of San Francisco shook for up to a minute. The terrible damage caused by the earthquake was made worse by raging fires, many of which came about because of overturned stoves. The fires burned for three days, and the disaster killed at least 3,000 people and left 225,000 homeless. Survivors did their best to find safe areas outside the city.

The Square Deal

President Theodore Roosevelt introduced a program of social reform that was known as the Square Deal. Roosevelt himself used the term after settling a miners' strike in 1902. He believed that industry and trade unions could get along together, so long as workers were treated fairly (given a "square deal"). This led to Congress establishing a Department of Commerce and Labor in 1903.

President Roosevelt stands next to a globe. His policy in foreign affairs was to "speak softly and carry a big stick," combining diplomacy with military strength.

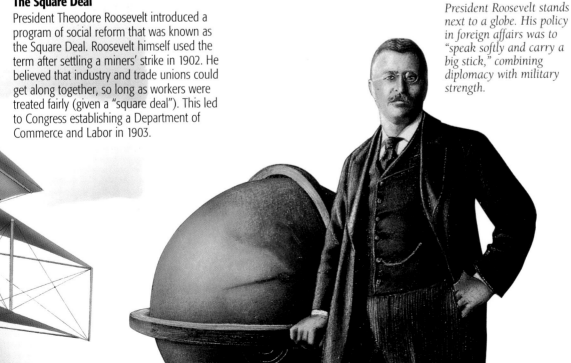

THE USA AT THE TURN OF THE CENTURY

1901
On 6 September, President William McKinley (1843–1901) is shot by anarchist Leon F. Czolgosz at the Pan American Exposition in Buffalo, New York; McKinley dies 8 days later.

1901–09
Presidency of Theodore Roosevelt (1858–1919).

1903
The US acquires construction rights to the Panama Canal after supporting a revolution in Panama that helped it gain independence from Colombia.

1907
Oklahoma becomes a state.

1908
A "gentlemen's agreement" is made between the US and Japan, reducing immigration but stopping discriminatory laws.

1912
Arizona and New Mexico become states.

1911
Anti-monopoly laws break up John D. Rockefeller's powerful Standard Oil Company.

1913
The US government gains the power to levy an income tax.

1914
The world's first airline operates flying-boat flights in Florida, USA, between St. Petersburg and Tampa.

1916
The first federal child labor law is passed by the US Congress, including a minimum working age of 14.

The Birth of Film

After the first public screening of moving pictures in Paris in 1895, filmmaking made great progress during the first twenty years of the 20th century. Movies became popular both in Europe and the United States. Talkies had not yet been invented, but the silent films were often accompanied by live music. Later, titles were inserted in scenes to show some dialogue. By 1915, film companies were all looking for star performers.

Helen Holmes prepares to leap onto a moving train in a trademark piece of athletic action.

American actress Lillian Gish (1893–1993) was one of the greatest stars of the silent screen.

Stunt Action

In the early days of film, actors performed their own stunts. This was a dangerous business. One of the best stunt-actresses was Helen Holmes (1893–1950), who began her film career in 1912. Two years later she starred in *The Hazards of Helen*, a series of 26 "thrill-a-minute" episodes. The heroine usually chased bad guys and had to jump on and off moving vehicles to catch them.

Special Effects

Filmmakers realized that they could make things more exciting by using special effects. In the early days, many effects were produced within the camera, or by using miniatures or back projection. French director Georges Méliès (1861–1938) experimented with movies, using a glass-enclosed studio for stop motion, superimposing images and other tricks. He also used color by hand-painting the film. Between 1899 and 1912 Méliès made more than 400 films.

A still from Georges Méliès' science-fiction film A Trip to the Moon (1902).

Silent Superstar

British-born American comedian Charlie Chaplin (1889–1977) took the world of silent comedy films by storm. He was enormously popular playing a likeable tramp dressed in baggy trousers, wearing a bowler hat and shuffling along in outsized shoes. Chaplin made *The Tramp* in 1915, and he was soon writing and directing as well as starring in his own films. Filmgoers called him "the funniest man in the world."

Charlie Chaplin in front of the camera as the tramp character he called "the little fellow."

A poster advertising
The Great Train Robbery.

Artistic Techniques

American director D. W. Griffith (1875–1948) used new techniques to improve silent films. He moved the camera much more than others, introducing shots from various angles and distances, including close-ups. His most famous film was *The Birth of a Nation* (1915), an epic about the American Civil War. The film was praised for its technique, but it was also criticized as being racist.

Poster for Cabiria *by Giovanni Pastrone (1914). It was second kolossal in the history of world cinema, after* Quo Vadis? *by Enrico Guazzoni (1876–1949).*

Still from The Birth of a Nation, *with Lillian Gish on the right. The film was more than two hours long and became a huge hit.*

Storytelling

In 1903, the American director Edwin S. Porter made one of the first films to tell a continuous story—all in 12 minutes. The action of *The Great Train Robbery* was "sensational and startling" (see poster, above). It showed the robbery itself, the robbers being chased, and their eventual capture. It set the scene for many Western films to come.

This nuclear model shows an atom's heavy, central nucleus surrounded by electrons, which travel around the nucleus at great speed.

Science and Technology

Great scientific advances were made in the early years of the 20th century. Those scientists who made the most revolutionary contributions were rewarded with a new honor—the Nobel Prize. Developments in physics and chemistry also led to medical advances, helping to treat disease and creating healthier living conditions for many people. In the field of engineering, motor cars became more widely available as new methods made them cheaper to produce.

A gramophone-record cover showing the importance of rail transport in 1900.

Nuclear Science

New Zealand-born physicist Ernest Rutherford (1871–1937) is often called the father of nuclear science. He discovered that atoms—the basic particles of all matter—have a nucleus at the center. In 1911 he put forward his own nuclear model of the atom, for which he is most famous. During the First World War, Rutherford worked on ways of detecting submarines.

Wireless Communication

Telegraph signals had been sent along wires since the 1830s, but at the beginning of the 20th century a new wireless form of communication was discovered. The Italian inventor and electrical engineer Guglielmo Marconi sent his first radio signals in 1895. Six years later, he transmitted a signal across the Atlantic Ocean (see map, right). The earliest practical use of the "wireless" (or radio) was communication with ships, and developing knowledge soon led to the first radio broadcasts for news and entertainment.

TRANSATLANTIC SIGNAL

From England to Newfoundland
Many scientists thought that because radio waves travel in a straight line, they could not be sent a long way because of the curvature of the earth. On 12 December 1901, Marconi proved them wrong. He repeatedly transmitted the three dots of the Morse code letter "S" from Poldhu, in Cornwall, to St. John's, in Newfoundland (Canada)— a distance of more than 2,100 miles (3,400 km).

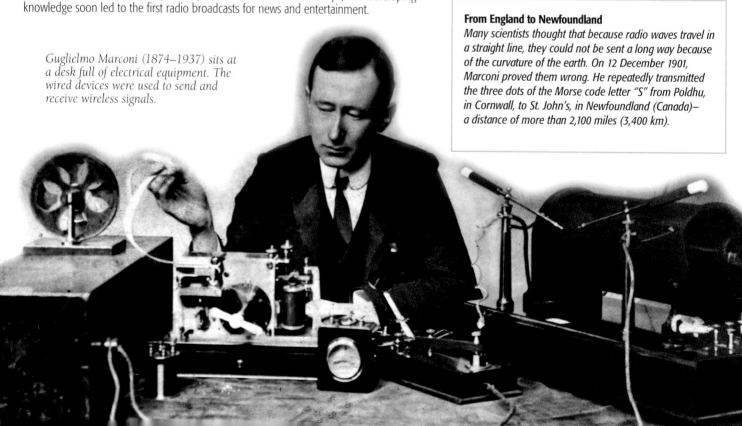

Guglielmo Marconi (1874–1937) sits at a desk full of electrical equipment. The wired devices were used to send and receive wireless signals.

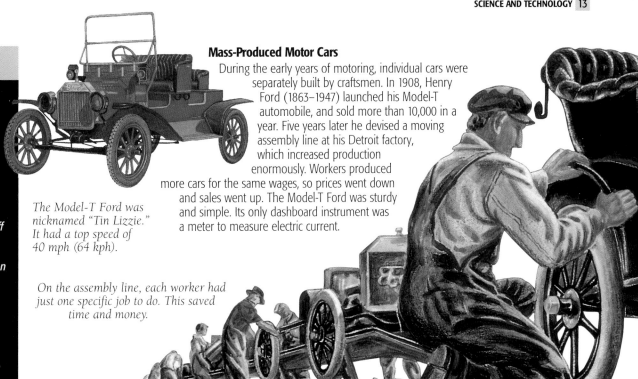

Mass-Produced Motor Cars

During the early years of motoring, individual cars were separately built by craftsmen. In 1908, Henry Ford (1863–1947) launched his Model-T automobile, and sold more than 10,000 in a year. Five years later he devised a moving assembly line at his Detroit factory, which increased production enormously. Workers produced more cars for the same wages, so prices went down and sales went up. The Model-T Ford was sturdy and simple. Its only dashboard instrument was a meter to measure electric current.

The Model-T Ford was nicknamed "Tin Lizzie." It had a top speed of 40 mph (64 kph).

On the assembly line, each worker had just one specific job to do. This saved time and money.

Nobel Prizes

Swedish businessman Alfred Nobel (1833–96) left a large sum of money to found annual awards for people who achieved great things "for the benefit of mankind." The first Nobel Prizes–for Chemistry, Physics, and Medicine or Physiology, as well as for Literature and Peace–were awarded in 1901. Polish-born French scientist Marie Curie won the 1903 physics prize (with her husband Pierre and Antoine Becquerel) for research on radiation. Eight years later she won the prize for chemistry on her own.

Marie Curie (1867–1934) made remarkable discoveries about radioactivity. She named the metallic element polonium after her native Poland.

Albert Einstein

Einstein was a German-born physicist, who became a Swiss citizen in 1905. In the same year he published a series of papers, with theories that showed new ways of thinking about time and space. Einstein's revolutionary theory of relativity said that while the speed of light is constant, time and motion are relative (or changeable) to an observer. Earlier scientists had insisted that time itself was always constant. Einstein widened the theory in 1916, and five years later received a Nobel Prize for Physics.

Albert Einstein (1879–1955), photographed in 1905. He worked in the Swiss patent office before he published his great theories.

Two British Kings

At the beginning of the 20th century, Britain was one of the world's most powerful nations. It had a vast empire and dominated areas of industry and commerce, including shipping and banking. The nation's foreign policy had been one of "splendid isolation," but now efforts were made to form alliances with Japan, France, and Russia. Edward VII, who succeeded Queen Victoria in 1901, made a significant contribution to British diplomacy in the years leading up to the First World War; his son, George V, had a less decisive role.

A three-handled Spode cup commemorating victories in the Boer War and declaring "Equal rights for all."

Edward VII, portrayed in royal regalia in 1902, the year of his coronation.

The Edwardian Age

Edward VII, whose reign became known as the Edwardian era, was a very popular king and a leader of British society. He enjoyed sports, and horses from the royal stables won the Derby three times. But he was also interested in foreign affairs, making an important official visit to France and later becoming the first reigning monarch to visit Russia.

Below: This postcard makes fun of the Entente Cordiale. It shows President Émile Loubet, followed by Edward VII and French foreign minister Théophile Delcassé.

Entente Cordiale

In 1904, France and Britain agreed to settle long-standing colonial disputes. The two countries reached an Entente Cordiale, or "friendly understanding." Among other things, they recognized each other's African interests, especially France's in Morocco and Britain's in Egypt. The agreement was not popular with Germany, which tried to put pressure on it, but only succeeded in strengthening the Anglo-French alliance.

Second Boer War

The British had fought the Boers (Dutch for "farmers") in 1881 for control of certain parts of southern Africa. Having lost territory then, the British fought the Dutch immigrants again from 1899 to 1902 in an attempt to take over the Boer republics of the Transvaal and Orange Free State. The British victors brutally herded many thousands of Boers into camps.

Prime Minister Asquith

Herbert Henry Asquith became prime minister in 1908. His Liberal government had an informal agreement of cooperation with the newly formed Labour Party and brought in important social reforms aimed at helping the working class. These included the Old Age Pension Act and increased taxes for the wealthy. Some reforms were resisted by the upper house of parliament (the House of Lords), and Asquith succeeded in reducing the Lords' power and opposition.

Portrait of Herbert Henry Asquith (1852–1928), who was prime minister until 1916. Later, he became the Earl of Oxford and Asquith.

THE BRITISH EMPIRE

Colonies Across the World

The map shows the extent of British colonial interests in 1912. Inherited from the Victorian era, these stretched from Canada to Australia and New Zealand. India and large parts of Africa were also still British. Other European powers were trying to expand their empires in Africa and Asia, leading to great rivalry.

George V comes to the throne

George V (1865–1936) was the second son of Edward VII, but became heir to the throne when his elder brother died in 1892. George became king on his father's death in 1910, and the following year he and his wife, Queen Mary, visited India and attended the Delhi Durbar, a splendid parade of imperial might. During the first few years of his reign, Germany began to build up its armaments.

A magnificent luncheon was held at the Guildhall in London to celebrate King George V's coronation.

BRITAIN BEFORE THE FIRST WORLD WAR

1901–10
Reign of Edward VII.

1902
The Peace of Vereeniging ends the second Boer War. An Anglo-Japanese Alliance is signed in London.

1902–05
Arthur Balfour (1848–1930) is Conservative prime minister of Britain.

1905–08
Henry Campbell-Bannerman (1836–1908) is Liberal prime minister, with Asquith in his cabinet.

1906
The Liberals win an important general election; the Labour Representation Committee (formed in 1900) is renamed the Labour Party.

1907
An Anglo-Russian agreement leads to the informal Triple Entente between France, Britain, and Russia.

1909
A Great Naval Review at Spithead (in the English Channel) shows off the powerful British fleet.

1911
The government's Parliamentary Act limits the power of the House of Lords.

Above and Below Stairs

During the Edwardian era, society in Britain and other European countries was strictly divided into classes. In the large houses of the upper class, the people who lived "below stairs"—the domestic servants who had their quarters in the basement—lived very different lives from those who employed them. While the wealthy enjoyed their exciting social lives, ordinary working-class people had very little free time, earned poorly, and often lived in squalid conditions.

These London families used any spare timber they could find for firewood.

A long-handled copper warming pan, which was filled with hot coals and used to warm a bed.

Edwardian High Society

The wealthy, influential members of Edwardian high society led busy social lives. Gentlemen went hunting, shooting, and fishing, and there were plenty of social occasions for ladies and gentlemen. Hostesses held large parties in their country houses, serving extravagant dinners with numerous dishes such as caviar, pheasant, and lobster on the menu. Such a dinner for 20 guests cost about £60 ($US118)—more than a maid earned in a year.

City Slums

Living conditions for working people in Edwardian cities such as London, Birmingham, Manchester, and Liverpool were often appalling. Coal-fired factories pumped out smoke, filling the city air with smog. There was a lack of housing for workers, leading to overcrowding and adding to problems of inadequate sanitation and the spread of disease. The Liberal government's reforms (see page 15) helped improve social services somewhat.

Fashion

Parisian fashion designers were prominent during the Belle Époque. Paul Poiret and others led a move toward longer, slimmer lines for women, with brighter colors. Simpler designs liberated wearers from the earlier tyranny of heavy corsets and were seen by some to reflect women's gradual emancipation. Fashion items included day dresses, walking dresses, tea gowns, evening gowns, shawls, coats, and capes.

This Edwardian bathing suit was a little less restricting than earlier Victorian models.

Parisian designers made ladies' dresses, like this one of 1909, slightly simpler than previously. Hats were always worn and were more elaborate than ever before.

Around 1912 dresses became more slender.

Domestic Service

Servants in the great houses of wealthy Edwardians worked long hours for low pay. Nevertheless, many working people considered it a privilege to serve the gentry. Girls often went into service from the age of 12, working at first as kitchen or scullery maids. They aimed to work their way up eventually to cook or housekeeper. In the servants' hall, there was just as strict an order of importance as above stairs.

In this painting, a housekeeper is seen apparently speaking severely to a maid and a footman.

The annual sailing regatta of Cowes Week, in early August, was an important event in the English social calendar.

Contrasting Pleasures

Dancing was important in all great European cities of the time. In forward-thinking Paris, ballet was revived as an art form by performers of the Ballets Russes and many famous artists designed their scenes. Vienna, then the capital of Austria-Hungary, was much more old-fashioned, and nineteenth-century waltzes were still popular among the aristocracy who dominated the city.

Costume designs by the Russian artist Léon Bakst for a Parisian ballet of 1911.

Gibson girls were outdoor, athletic types. They showed a spirit of adventure with a touch of mischief.

Gibson Girls

American illustrator Charles D. Gibson (1867–1944) was a specialist in pen-and-ink drawing. His illustrations of attractive, fun-loving young women appeared in weekly journals around the turn of the century and were extremely popular. The "Gibson girls", as they were known, were seen as the American ideal of fashionable femininity. They captured the spirit of the age.

Women Before the War

Roles and opportunities for women began to change during the early years of the 20th century. Some women started to find work as typists and telephonists, while others found careers as writers. Votes for women had been secured in New Zealand in 1893, and women's movements gradually made greater political demands in other countries around the world. In Britain, a growing number of suffragettes overcame harsh treatment to make progress possible for women of all social classes.

WOMEN BEFORE THE WAR

1902
Australia gives women the right to vote in national elections.

1903
Emmeline Pankhurst and daughter Christabel found the National Women's Social and Political Union.

1906
Finland becomes the first European country to give women the vote.

1907
Finland has the world's first female members of parliament. The American Equality League of Self-Supporting Women is founded.

1913
Women gain the vote in Norway. The British "Cat and Mouse Act" allows the temporary release from prison of suffragettes whose health is in danger from hunger striking. Suffragette Emily Davison deliberately runs in front of a horse owned by King George V at the Derby race and is killed.

1914
Beatrice Webb and her husband Sidney join the Labour Party.

Suffragettes

The suffragettes were women who sought the right to vote in political elections (this right is called suffrage). From 1903 they organized demonstrations, chained themselves to railings and used other forms of protest to try and get women the vote. In Britain, they were led by Emmeline Pankhurst (1858–1928). She and her daughters Christabel and Sylvia were treated harshly by the authorities and imprisoned. Many suffragette prisoners who went on hunger strike were force-fed.

Members of the suffragette movement celebrate their release from prison in 1908. It was another 20 years before British women got full voting rights.

German score of a 1913 operetta, The Ideal Wife, featuring the tango, which was clearly a big selling point.

Dance Crazes

Dance music was very popular throughout the period. The favorite form of piano music was ragtime, which influenced the development of jazz. Wind-up gramophones were becoming popular, so young people could play music to dance to, as well as going to dance halls. From 1910 a new dance came from Argentina to the United States and Europe—the tango. This dance involved a close embrace that shocked many older people at the time.

Rosa Luxemburg

Many women took part in revolutionary politics. Polish-born German communist Rosa Luxemburg (1871–1919) followed the teachings of Karl Marx. She helped found the Polish Social Democratic Party and, later, the German Communist Party. From 1907 to 1914 she taught at the Social Democratic Party School in Berlin. "Bloody Rosa," as she was sometimes called, was a great believer in the power of mass strikes.

Rosa Luxemburg was a powerful speaker and writer. She urged workers to take political power into their own hands.

This stained-glass window commemorating the Fabian Society was commissioned by dramatist George Bernard Shaw in 1910.

Beatrice Webb

The English socialist Beatrice Webb (1858–1943) came from a wealthy background. A great believer in equality and democracy, she became a social worker in London, where her experiences among poor people underlined her beliefs. She joined the socialist Fabian Society and married one of its executive members, Sidney Webb. Beatrice served on a royal commission investigating poverty in Britain. Together, Beatrice and Sidney established the political journal *New Statesman*.

Scott of the Antarctic

British naval officer Captain Robert Falcon Scott (1868–1912) led two expeditions to Antarctica. He sailed south first in *Discovery* (1900–04) and then in *Terra Nova* (1910–12). The second expedition turned into a so-called "Race to the South Pole" with Amundsen (see below). Scott reached the Pole in January 1912, only to find that he had been beaten to it. He and his four companions died on the return journey.

Roald Amundsen

Norwegian explorer Roald Amundsen (1872–1928) had great success in both polar regions. In 1903–06 he was first to sail through the Northwest Passage, the Arctic sea route leading from the Atlantic to the Pacific Ocean. Five years later Amundsen became the first man to reach the South Pole—on December 14, 1911—beating Scott by 5 weeks.

Amundsen (on the left, with one of his team of four) carries out a survey at the southernmost point on Earth.

Captain Scott in his winter base, during his second and last expedition to Antarctica.

EXPEDITIONS AND DISCOVERIES

1900
British archeologist Sir Arthur Evans begins excavating the Palace of Minos at Knossos, Crete.

1901
French archeologist Jacques de Morgan discovers a stone pillar in Susa, Persia, with the law code of Hammurabi, an ancient Babylonian ruler.

1905–08
Swedish geographer Sven Hedin explores and maps the Trans-Himalaya mountain range of Tibet.

1907
Hungarian-British geographer Sir Aurel Stein discovers the Cave of the Thousand Buddhas in China.

1911
French pilot Roland Garros sets a new altitude record in a Blériot XI plane of 12,828 feet (3,910 m).

Exploration and Discovery

During the previous century many of the great European explorers had concentrated on Africa and the tropical regions of the world. At the beginning of the 1900s the polar regions were left as some of the world's least explored areas. This caused races to the North and South Poles that led to well-documented stories of hardship and heroism. In Asia and South America, archeologists were making further astonishing discoveries about the world's earlier civilizations.

To the North Pole

American explorer Robert Peary led an expedition to Greenland in 1891, with his wife Josephine, colleague Matthew Henson, and future rival Frederick Cook. Eighteen years later—on April 6, 1909—Peary and Henson, along with four Inuit helpers, arrived at the North Pole. Then Peary learned that Cook claimed to have reached the Pole a year earlier. This was disputed, and experts credit Peary with having been first.

Robert Peary (1856–1920) learned his Arctic skills, including clothing, diet, and dog-handling, from the Inuit people.

Lost City of the Incas

American archeologist Hiram Bingham (1875–1956) taught Latin American history at Yale University. But he liked to be thought of as an explorer rather than an academic. In July 1911, Native American guides led him to an overgrown site in the Andes mountains of Peru. Bingham had been searching for remains of the Inca people, whose empire had been destroyed by invading Europeans in the 16th century. He soon realized from the wonderful stonework he saw that he had rediscovered an Inca city with a sacred plaza and a circular temple.

When Bingham discovered the Inca city, called Machu Picchu, it was overgrown. Today, the cleared and excavated site is a great tourist attraction.

Harriet Quimby's trademark flight suit was made of purple satin.

Harriet
Quimby
Pioneer
Pilot

USAirmail
50

Trans-Antarctic Expedition

Sir Ernest Shackleton (1874–1922) was on Captain Scott's first polar expedition, and Shackleton almost reached the South Pole himself in 1909. On his British Imperial Trans-Antarctic Expedition of 1914–16, Shackleton's ship *Endurance* got stuck in the ice and was eventually crushed. He and his crew drifted for five months on ice floes before reaching Elephant Island by sledge and boat. Shackleton then sailed for 800 miles (1,300 km) to find help. He died in the Antarctic at the start of his next expedition.

This photograph shows some of Shackleton's dogs beside his ice-wrecked ship.

Aviation Pioneer

In 1911, aviatrix Harriet Quimby became the first American woman to receive a pilot's licence. She soon became the first woman to make a night-time flight and, in 1912, the first female pilot to fly across the English Channel. She made the flight in a plane designed by Louis Blériot, who had achieved the feat two years earlier. Quimby's flight lasted 59 minutes. Later in the year, she was killed at the Boston Aviation Meeting when her plane crashed.

The Titanic eases its way out of Southampton dock on 10 April 1912, at the start of its maiden voyage.

The Titanic Sinks

The Titanic was a famous luxury liner that struck an iceberg and sank in the Atlantic Ocean in 1912. More than 1,500 people died in the disaster, which happened on the ship's maiden voyage from Southampton to New York. Following an inquiry, new safety rules were brought in concerning lifeboats, use of radio, and speed in icy seas. The wreck of the Titanic was found in 1985. It was lying on the ocean floor at a depth of about 13,120 feet (4,000 m).

White Star Line logo.

The "Unsinkable" Liner

The Titanic was the largest ocean liner afloat. It was 882 feet (269 m) long and 92 feet (28 m) wide, and was thought to be unsinkable because its hull was divided into 16 watertight compartments. Little thought was given to collisions. Yet shortly after leaving dock in Southampton, the Titanic's enormous swell caused problems to another liner and the two ships missed each other by little more than a yard.

The Ill-fated Night

Shortly before midnight on April 14, when the Titanic was about 400 miles (640 km) southeast of Newfoundland, lookouts saw an iceberg straight ahead. But the ship was traveling fast—at about 21 knots (24 mph/39 kph)—and hit the iceberg. Though it was a glancing blow, it made cracks in the ship's steel hull. Water poured in and started to flood six of the 16 compartments in the ship's hull. The Titanic was doomed, and less than three hours later it sank beneath the waves.

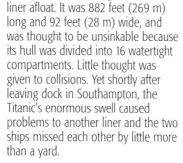

The first lifeboats left the ship at 12:45 a.m. Organization was poor and many of the lifeboats were not even full.

Three Classes

Of the 1,316 passengers, about a quarter were in luxurious first-class cabins on the upper and promenade decks. These cost £870 for a one-way voyage. A smaller number were in less expensive second class. More than half the passengers were in steerage—third-class cabins shared by up to 8 people, each paying £7 and 10 shillings. Most steerage passengers were on a one-way ticket to the United States in search of a new life.

Captain and Crew

The Titanic had 913 crew members. The captain of the ship, 62-year-old Edward J. Smith, was on his last voyage before retiring. He had seven officers, who were in charge of deck crew, engineers, stewards, restaurant staff, and musicians. Twenty-three female crew members served as stewardesses and cashiers. There were two radio operators, who repeatedly sent distress signals. Unfortunately the nearest ship, the Californian, had switched its radio off for the night. Another ship, the Carparthia, picked up the signal but could only arrive about 4 hours later.

Kate Winslet played a wealthy passenger in Titanic, a 1997 film based on the disaster.

The captain (in the front row, third from left), along with his officers and the ship's chief purser, who was responsible for passengers' welfare.

A telegram announcing that one of the passengers (W.H. Stead) survived the disaster.

THE TITANIC SINKS

1909
Construction of the Titanic begins at a shipyard in Belfast.

1911
The ship's hull is launched on 31 May.

1912
April 10
12:00 The Titanic leaves Southampton.
18:30 Arrives at Cherbourg, France; picks up more passengers.

April 11,
11:30 Arrives at Queenstown, Ireland; leaves at 13:55.

April 14,
11:40 The Titanic strikes an iceberg.

April 15,
12:10 Radio operator sends the first distress signal.
12:25 The first lifeboats are loaded with women and children.
12:55 Distress rockets are fired.
2:05 The stern of the ship rises very steeply; the last lifeboat leaves.
2:20 The ship breaks in two, its lights go out, and it quickly sinks.
4:10 The first lifeboat is picked up by the Carpathia.

Human Tragedy

The Titanic had 20 lifeboats, enough for just over half the 2,229 on board. This was the main reason that less than a third of the total number survived. Those who jumped into the sea quickly froze to death in the icy water. Of the women and children among the passengers, over two thirds were rescued by the *Carpathia*. The captain went down with his ship. After this disaster, it was made compulsory for ships to have a lifeboat space for every person on board.

A pot of shaving cream was found amongst the floating wreckage.

Asia in the Early 20th Century

There were major developments in the largest and most powerful Asian countries during this period. The Qing Dynasty lost power in China, and revolution led to the setting up of a republic. In India, British colonial control was coming under pressure from Hindu and Muslim nationalists. Meanwhile, imperial Japan became the first Asian nation to defeat a European power (Russia) in war and was able to expand its colonies.

In 1901 the Boxer rebels were rounded up. Many were shot.

Empress Dowager Cixi embezzled funds to restore the Imperial Summer Palace, including this marble boat.

The Boxer Rebellion

In 1900, a group of Chinese rebels rose against Westerners, including Christian missionaries and their Chinese converts. Called Boxers from the name of their secret society, the Righteous and Harmonious Fists, the rebels marched on Beijing. They burned houses and schools, attacking anyone who supported foreigners. A year later, the rebellion was crushed by an international force of troops from eight different nations.

Japanese flags were flown to celebrate a great victory over Russia.

Empress Dowager Cixi

During the reign of the Manchu emperor Guangxu, from 1875 to 1908, Guangxu's adoptive mother Cixi acted as regent. She dominated the Chinese government and prevented the young emperor from modernizing the fading imperial system. Previously consort of one emperor and then mother of another, the empress dowager resisted reform, holding back China's opportunity for peaceful change. In 1908, on her deathbed, Cixi ordered that the emperor be poisoned.

Russo-Japanese War

The Russo-Japanese War of 1904–05 arose from the countries' conflicting interests in Manchuria. The Japanese used modern equipment and superior leadership to defeat the Russian land forces and Baltic fleet. Their victory inspired other colonized peoples as the first example of an Asian nation defeating a European power. At the resulting peace conference in New Hampshire, USA, Japan gained control of southern Manchuria and Korea.

Revolution in China

In 1905, Chinese revolutionary organizations formed a United League, choosing Sun Yat-sen as their leader. Over the next six years, the rebels attacked the Manchu imperial government, but without success. Finally, in 1911, a revolutionary group managed to overthrow the provincial government in Wuhan. This signalled the end of the Qing dynasty of the Manchus, as other Chinese provinces declared their republican independence.

Former army leader Yuan Shikai was the first president of the Republic of China from 1912 to 1916.

Tiger hunting was popular among British colonials in India.

Ito Hirobumi

Elder statesman Ito had been Japanese premier four times before he was made resident general in Korea in 1905. He helped modernize Japan, stressing cooperation between politicians and bureaucrats. However, he never gained the trust of the Koreans. In October 1909 Ito was assassinated in Harbin, China, by three bullets from the gun of a young Korean nationalist. The following year, Japan took full control of Korea.

Portrait of Ito Hirobumi (1841–1909), who was made a Japanese prince in 1907.

British India

In 1905, the division of the province of Bengal into separate Hindu and Muslim sections led to violent protests. This persuaded the British to appoint an Indian national to the viceroy's executive council, and in 1911 Bengal was reunited. Three years later, Indian troops were fighting for Britain against Germany. Nevertheless, Indian politicians kept up their demands for reform.

Last Chinese Emperor

Cixi had ordered that the former Qing emperor's nephew, Pu Yi, take the throne. He did so, two months short of his third birthday. The boy was taken from his mother and installed in the Forbidden City in Beijing. His father acted as regent, but Pu Yi was worshiped in the same way as all previous Chinese emperors. Revolutionaries forced him to give up the throne at the age of six.

Pu Yi, as he was portrayed in the film The Last Emperor *(1987).*

Ottoman Decline, Balkan Wars

The Ottoman Empire had become smaller and weaker during the previous century. In 1878 it lost Bulgaria to the Russians, and in 1897 the Greeks declared war following an uprising in Crete. Montenegro, Romania and Serbia also gained their independence. As their power declined, the Ottoman Turks saw it in their interest to side with Germany in the First World War. Except for Bulgaria, their former Balkan provinces continued to fight the Ottomans on behalf of the Allies.

DECLINE OF THE OTTOMAN EMPIRE

Ottoman Empire 1800

Ottoman territory lost 1805–1914

Ottoman Empire 1914

Losing European Territory

In 1908 King Ferdinand of Bulgaria declared his country's full independence from the Ottoman Empire. Adding to the earlier loss of former provinces, by 1914 this left the Ottomans with eastern Thrace (modern European Turkey) as their only European possession. The map shows how the Ottoman Empire shrank in size.

Young Turks

Turkish revolutionary groups opposed the tyrannical Ottoman sultan, Abdul Hamid II. In 1908 a group called the Committee of Union and Progress, with members known as the Young Turks, led a revolt. They first forced the sultan to restore parliament, and then deposed him. Their aim was to return the Ottoman Empire to its former greatness, and their success led to some modern reforms. They introduced a spirit of Turkish nationalism, but their foreign policies were misguided.

Abdul Hamid II (1842–1918) was Ottoman sultan from 1876 to 1909. He opposed, although not very effectively, all Western interference in Ottoman affairs.

New Alliances

In order to try and achieve the aims of the Young Turks, the Ottoman Empire allied itself with Germany in August 1914. Fearing that the Armenians in the northeast of the empire would support Russia instead, the Ottoman government in 1915 (and later) deported about 1,750,000 Armenians to Syria and Mesopotamia. Hundreds of thousands died on the way. Bulgaria also joined Germany in the Great War, hoping to regain territory lost in the Second Balkan War (see page 27).

The Greek battleship Georgios Averof steams into Constantinople in 1918. The Greeks joined the Great War on the side of the Allies in 1917.

Peoples of the Region

Most of the Balkan nations had been part of the Ottoman Empire for hundreds of years. But there were many different ethnic groups, cultures and languages within the nations, which caused tensions. Kurdish efforts towards self-government were crushed by the Turks early in the 20th century.

Croat

Bulgarian

Albanian

Kurdish

Habsburg emperor Franz Josef (reigned 1848–1916) discusses Austro-Hungarian foreign policy.

Bosnia-Herzegovina

Since 1878 Bosnia-Herzegovina had been controlled by Austria-Hungary. In 1908 the empire formally annexed the region, causing unrest among Serb and Slav nationalists. The military governor of Bosnia dissolved parliament and declared a state of emergency. The heir to the imperial throne visited the Bosnian capital of Sarajevo and was killed (see page 30). His death started a train of events that soon resulted in the outbreak of the Great War.

Lawrence of Arabia

In 1916, British army officer T. E. Lawrence (1888–1935) joined the Arab revolt against the Ottoman Turks. Lawrence helped the Arabs wage a successful guerrilla war against the Ottomans, by wrecking trains and other tactics. In this way the Arabs prevented thousands of Turkish troops from taking part in the Palestine campaign, helping the Allies. Lawrence led a triumphant Arab force into Damascus in October, 1918.

Thomas Edward Lawrence wrote of his exploits in The Seven Pillars of Wisdom.

Balkan Wars

In the First Balkan War (1912–13), Serbia, Bulgaria, Greece and Montenegro formed an alliance against the Ottoman Empire. This Balkan League had a force of 750,000 men that overpowered the Ottomans, who lost almost all their European possessions. When the victors disagreed over territory, Bulgaria began the Second Balkan War (1913) by attacking Serbia and Greece. The Bulgarians were defeated and again lost much of the land they had just gained.

Ferdinand, king of Bulgaria, walks over captured flags during the First Balkan War.

War Plans and Weapons

From the beginning of the century the major European powers steadily built up military power, strengthening alliances and making plans for war. Germany had a large, well-trained army and was gaining a powerful naval force. Russia made plans to mobilize its forces against both Germany and Austria-Hungary. The destructive power of all the armies was increased by new weapons, including machine guns and giant howitzers.

Heavy machine guns generally fired about 450 rounds of ammunition per minute.

Admiral Sir John Jellicoe, commander of the British Grand Fleet from 1914.

Essen in the Ruhr Valley was the centre of German industrial might. Its factories produced steel and many of Germany's weapons.

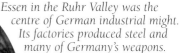

Sea Power

When Britain launched its large, fast, heavily armed battleship Dreadnought in 1906, it gave the Royal Navy a huge advantage over Germany and Austria-Hungary. This revolutionary vessel was built in a record 14 months. Germany responded quickly. By 1914 the German navy had 14 large battleships to Britain's 20. Battleships were protected at sea by smaller destroyers and cruisers, and the Royal Navy had more of these vessels too.

Dreadnought was 526 feet (160 m) long and had a speed of 22 knots (41 kph).

GERMANY'S SCHLIEFFEN PLAN

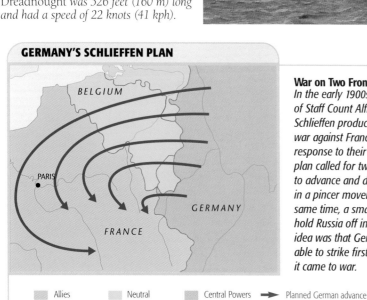

BELGIUM

PARIS

GERMANY

FRANCE

 Allies   Neutral   Central Powers   ➡ Planned German advance

War on Two Fronts

In the early 1900s, German Chief of Staff Count Alfred von Schlieffen produced a plan for war against France and Russia in response to their alliance. The plan called for two military wings to advance and defeat the French in a pincer movement. (At the same time, a smaller army would hold Russia off in the east.) The idea was that Germany would be able to strike first and decisively if it came to war.

France's Plan XVII

Plan XVII was adopted in 1913 by commander-in-chief Marshal Joffre, who pushed hard for increased military spending in France so that the French armies would be ready to mobilize and prepared for the defence of France. Once the war broke out, France took the opportunity to advance into Alsace and Lorraine, which it had lost to Germany in 1871.

COLONIAL EMPIRES IN 1914

GREENLAND

CANADA

RUSSIA

BRITAIN
GERMANY
FRANCE
SPAIN

CHINA

JAPAN

USA

AFRICA

INDIA

AUSTRALIA

British · Italian · Portuguese · Belgian
French · Russian · Japanese · American (USA)
German · Dutch · Spanish · Danish

An Imperial Age

In 1914 the British Empire still covered almost a quarter of the globe, and Britain knew that it could count on its colonies in time of war. The Russian Empire was vast, but much of its Asian territory in Siberia was unpopulated. The Europeans had divided up Africa between them. As war approached, there was little to suggest that the age of empires was almost over.

Germans are mobilized in Berlin and head off to the Western Front by train.

Vital Railways

Throughout Europe, railways formed a vital supply route. Troops were deployed and then supplied by train, so railway networks and timetables helped shape the military build-up. Military authorities took over rail use for mass mobilization. The British army, for example, formed a Railway Operating Division. Tracks were essential for troop movements, therefore their destruction would cause great problems for advancing troops. So once war began, attackers could be quickly cut off from reinforcements and supplies, giving an advantage to well-supplied defenders.

The M11 howitzer was developed at the Skoda works in Pilsen in 1906. It was built secretly and was ready for action by the Austro-Hungarian and German armies in 1914. Nicknamed "Schlanke Emma" ("Slender Emma"), this giant weapon could fire shells to a range of 7 miles (11 km).

War Breaks Out

By 1914 the political alliances among European nations, along with increased nationalism and military build-up, made for an extremely tense situation. War was finally triggered by the assassination of the heir to the Austro-Hungarian throne, which led to the alliances being called to action. Five weeks after the assassination, German troops were invading neutral Belgium. Politicians and the public on both sides hoped the war would be short, but military experts feared the reverse.

Franz Ferdinand (1863–1914) and his wife, Countess Sophie, were both killed by the assassin's bullets.

Assassination in Sarajevo

Archduke Franz Ferdinand, heir to the Austro-Hungarian throne, visited Bosnia (then a region of his empire). There he was shot dead by Gavrilo Princip, a member of a group called Young Bosnia (which was being exploited by a Serbian nationalist group, the Black Hand). The nationalists were protesting against the oppression of Bosnian Serbs. The assassination led to demands within Austria-Hungary for an attack on Serbia, which gained backing from the German Kaiser. The Serb capital Belgrade was bombarded a month later.

On Other Fronts

When the German navy attacked Russian bases in the Black Sea in October 1914, the Allies came to Russia's support and declared war on the Ottoman Empire. The Ottomans blocked the sea route to southern Russia, and British and French warships attacked the Dardanelles strait. The following year, Australian, New Zealand, British and French troops landed on the Gallipoli Peninsula in Turkey, but the campaign ended in failure with great loss of life.

Field Marshal Paul von Hindenburg (middle, foreground) and General Erich Ludendorff (to his left) were hailed as heroes in Germany after victories on the Eastern Front.

Germany Battles on Two Fronts

In the west, the German army swept into neutral Belgium in August 1914 and headed towards France, causing Britain to declare war on Germany. The powerful German offensive led to great battles along the Western Front (see Marne, opposite). In the east, Russian troops invaded German territory faster than expected. But their armies became separated, and the Germans won a great victory at the Battle of Tannenberg (in East Prussia).

Major Offensives

On the Eastern Front, the Russians had many more troops than the Germans, but their equipment was inferior. Russian communications were also less effective, and the Germans followed up Tannenberg with another victory at the Masurian Lakes (in present-day northern Poland). By the end of 1914, trench warfare had been established on this front.

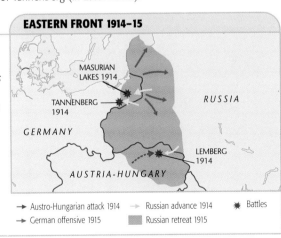

EASTERN FRONT 1914–15

MASURIAN LAKES 1914

TANNENBERG 1914

RUSSIA

GERMANY

LEMBERG 1914

AUSTRIA-HUNGARY

→ Austro-Hungarian attack 1914   → Russian advance 1914   ✳ Battles
→ German offensive 1915   ▨ Russian retreat 1915

An ANZAC (Australian and New Zealand Army Corps) soldier. More than 11,000 ANZAC troops were killed at Gallipoli.

First Battle of the Marne

By early September 1914, German troops had reached the River Marne, just 30 miles (50 km) east of Paris. Then General Joffre launched a French counterattack, supported by the British Expeditionary Force. Fierce fighting stopped the breakthrough, and the German troops started to withdraw. Eventually they retreated about 40 miles (65 km). It was a victory for the Allies, but the German army was not beaten. The Marne battle showed that this was not going to be a short war.

German biplanes fly over the River Marne. During the famous battle of 1914, the French army suffered 250,000 casualties.

THE WAR IN 1914

1914
June 28
Archduke Franz Ferdinand is assassinated in Sarajevo.

July 23
Austria-Hungary issues an ultimatum to Serbia.

July 28
Austria-Hungary declares war on Serbia.

August 1–3
Germany declares war on Russia and then France.

August 4
German troops invade Belgium. Britain declares war on Germany.

August 10
Austria-Hungary invades Russia, starting war on the Eastern Front.

September 6–10
First Battle of the Marne.

September 11
The Austro-Hungarians are forced by Russia to begin withdrawal from Galicia.

November 1–5
Russia and Allies declare war on Ottoman Empire.

December 15
Austro-Hungarians withdraw from Belgrade.

Peace Protests

Not everyone agreed with the war. In 1914 many women who had been campaigning for equal rights (see page 18) turned their attention to the struggle for peace. The following year about 1,300 women from Europe and North America formed the Women's International League for Peace and Freedom in the neutral Netherlands.

Women campaigned in their own peace movement.

Opposing Sides

T he two opposing sides in the Great War, as it was known at the time, were made up of alliances between different empires and nations. They formed the Central and Allied Powers. Though it came to be known later as a "world war," most of the fighting was carried out by land armies in Europe. Other countries outside Europe (including the Ottoman Empire on one side and the Asian part of the Russian Empire on the other) were drawn in by imperial or political alliance.

This poster shows the uniforms and flags of the four members of the Central Powers: Austria-Hungary, Germany, Ottoman Empire (Turkey) and Bulgaria.

Central Powers

The Dual Monarchy of Austria-Hungary was led by the Habsburg ruler, Franz Josef (1830–1916), who was Emperor of Austria and King of Hungary. Austria-Hungary had formed an alliance with the newly formed German Empire in 1882. The Ottoman Empire, led by the Sultan of Turkey, made a defensive alliance with Germany in July, 1914. Bulgaria (a former province of the Ottoman Empire) joined the Central Powers in the following year.

The Allies

The first countries to join Serbia as Allies included the Triple Entente powers (see page 15) of Britain, France and Russia. Colonies in the British Empire joined the UK in war. Japan also joined in 1914 because of its alliance with Britain, and many countries from around the world joined the Allies over the next four years (see table). The United States was at first neutral, but crucially became an "associated power" in April 1917.

Wilhelm II (1859–1941)
was the eldest son of
Frederick III and
Princess Victoria,
daughter of Queen
Victoria of England.

An American army
recruit signs up and
collects his uniform.
Conscription was
introduced in the United
States in May, 1917.

The Kaiser

Kaiser Wilhelm II was German emperor from 1888 to 1918. The last ruler of the Hohenzollern dynasty, he was a cousin of both George V of England and Nicholas II of Russia. His education had included military training, and he built up Germany's army and navy. As head of state, he was also commander-in-chief of the German armed forces.

Kitchener's Call to Arms

Horatio Herbert Kitchener (1850–1916) was appointed British Secretary of State for war in 1914. A distinguished soldier and field marshal himself, Lord Kitchener showed such determination that it made him a symbol of the British will to win. Though he believed in conscription, he accepted Prime Minister Asquith's belief that this was impossible before 1916. Kitchener therefore set about recruiting and organizing a mass volunteer army.

Printed by the Victoria House Printi

A German infantryman with the old-style spiked helmet, which was replaced with a rounded steel version in 1916.

A French infantryman with a standard-issue Lebel rifle and bayonet.

Infantry

Infantrymen (foot soldiers) formed the armies' basic assault weapon. They carried a rifle, which could be fitted with a bayonet for use in close combat. Infantry commanders in 1914 tended to believe they could be successful without the need for artillery support. However, the experience of war taught them that a more cautious advance, designed to break down well-protected, established defenses, was more likely to be successful, particularly if it was well prepared and supported by heavy artillery.

This famous recruitment poster, showing the face of Lord Kitchener, first appeared in the London Opinion magazine in 1914.

DIVIDED EUROPE

NORWAY
SWEDEN
DENMARK
RUSSIA
GREAT BRITAIN
HOLLAND GERMANY
Neutral countries
BELGIUM
POLAND
Battlefront
LUXEMBOURG
LORRAINE
ALSACE
UKRAINE
FRANCE
AUSTRIA-HUNGARY
ROMANIA
SPAIN
ITALY
SERBIA BULGARIA
MONTENEGRO
ALBANIA
OTTOMAN EMPIRE
PORTUGAL
GIBRALTAR (British)
GREECE
PALESTINE
MALTA (British)
CYPRUS (British)
LIBYA (to Italy)
EGYPT (British Protectorate)

Central Powers	Allies	Allies
Germany	Great Britain	Belgium
Austria-Hungary	France	Italy
Bulgaria	Russia	Romania
Ottoman Empire	Serbia	Portugal

Allies, Central Powers and Neutrals

This map of allegiances shows how the Central Powers were surrounded by the Allies, apart from in the southeast (the Ottoman Empire) and the north (neutral countries). The Scandinavian nations remained neutral, though the Norwegian merchant fleet carried Allied cargo and was badly damaged. Neutral Spain sold goods to the warring nations. The yellow lines show the main fronts (or battle lines).

Trench Systems

Frontline trenches—nearest the enemy—were usually zigzagged and had barbed wire in front. They were reached by small passages from support trenches, where men could rest when they were not on duty. Further back were reserve trenches. The two sides' frontline trenches were separated by a "no-man's-land," which varied in width from tens to hundreds of meters. When one side launched an attack, soldiers had to go "over the top" and rush towards the enemy.

Both sides used sharp-shooting snipers to pick off any enemy soldier who appeared above the parapet of his trench.

Some deep trenches were lined with timber. Soldiers on duty had to watch out for snipers.

Defense in Depth

The German army built deep systems of trenches along the Western Front. From 1915, the Germans used concrete to strengthen fortified areas and dug deep bombardment shelters. Their systems included second-line trenches, and in 1916 large defensive trenches formed a system known as the Hindenburg Line. German defense in depth meant that the Allies suffered great casualties when they advanced and tried to capture line after line of trenches.

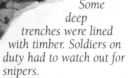

Field telephones like this one were used for communication, and there were a small number of wireless sets.

War in the Air

At the beginning of the war, aviation was still in its infancy. Britain, France, Germany and Russia were all adding air units to their armies, using planes to observe enemy movements on the ground and then dropping bombs by hand. By 1916, fighter planes were taking part in close-combat dogfights, trying to shoot each other down with machine guns. As aircraft improved, flying faster and higher, whole squadrons took part in these air battles.

The British Sopwith Camel fighter biplane had two sets of wings and two machine guns. It had a top speed of 115 mph (185 kph).

Trench Warfare and Dogfights

Trench warfare was a major feature of the Great War. On both sides, a battalion of men would serve a spell at the front, then a period in support, followed by time in reserve. After a short rest, the cycle of trench duty would start all over again. There were huge casualties on both sides along the Western Front. The increased use of aircraft made trenches even more dangerous places to be.

Christmas Truce

On the first Christmas Eve of the war, British troops on the Western Front heard their enemies singing German carols. The British joined in with their own songs, as guns on both sides gradually fell silent. Some opposing soldiers met up in "no-man's-land" and there was even an informal international game of soccer. This friendly ceasefire was totally unofficial, and top commanders frowned on it.

During the unofficial truce, German and British soldiers shook hands.

Poison Gas

The use of lethal chlorine gas by the Germans in April 1915 caused total panic, as Allied troops suffocated in seconds. The gas was released from canisters, but a changing wind could damage the attackers too, as happened to the British when they first used it. Later, mustard gas was also employed and was even added to high-explosive shells. The German army used most gas, followed by the French and the British.

Gas masks were introduced by both sides to protect their troops.

Baron Manfred von Richthofen (1892–1918) got his colorful nickname, the Red Baron, because of his squadron's red planes.

The Red Baron

German flying ace Manfred von Richthofen, known as the Red Baron, was the war's top-scoring pilot. He shot down 80 enemy aircraft, five more than René Fonck of France. Von Richthofen served first as a cavalry officer, before joining the German Army Air Service. He became commander of Fighter Group 1, and was killed when his plane was shot down by ground fire during a dogfight in the last year of the war.

A German Fokker Dr-1 triplane (with three sets of wings), as flown by the Red Baron. This single-seat fighter had the same top speed as the Sopwith Camel.

New Mobile Weapons

In 1915 the British developed a new weapon, which they called a "landship," but code-named "tank" because it looked like a water tank. The code-name stuck, and the first tanks went into production. These new armored combat vehicles traveled on caterpillar tracks and were ideal for trench warfare. The French army also developed and used them successfully, but the Germans did not introduce theirs until 1918 and made very few.

Some early tanks had a machine gun in a revolving turret. Small tanks could smash through barbed wire, but had trouble crossing wide trenches. Larger versions were soon developed.

TRENCH WARFARE AND DOGFIGHTS

1915
On April 22, the Germans use poison gas against Allied lines (French and Algerian troops) in the Second Battle of Ypres; the British retaliate on September 25 at the Artois-Loos offensive. Dutch designer Anthony Fokker, working for Germany, develops a machine gun that times shots between an aircraft's spinning propeller blades.

1916
By February, the Aéronautique Militaire (French air force) has 1,149 aircraft. In August, Manfred von Richthofen becomes a fighter pilot on the Western Front; the German Army Air Service forms specialist fighter units. On September 15, Britain brings the first tanks into action during the Battle of the Somme.

1917
On April 26, a great dogfight takes place between a total of 94 British and German aircraft. In July, the Sopwith Camel goes into full service with the British Royal Flying Corps. On November 20, 474 British tanks break through German lines in the Battle of Cambrai.

1918
On April 1, the British air services unite as the Royal Air Force. In August, Canadian fighter ace Billy Bishop (who shot down 72 German aircraft) joins the British Air Ministry. In September, US officer Billy Mitchell commands the largest air assault (1,500 Allied aircraft) in a mission over German lines in France.

Women and the Home Front

PUBLIC WARNING

The public are advised to familiarise themselves with the appearance of British and German Airships and Aeroplanes, so that they may not be alarmed by British aircraft, and may take shelter if German aircraft appear. Should hostile aircraft be seen, take shelter immediately in the nearest available house, preferably in the basement, and remain there until the aircraft have left the vicinity : do not stand about in crowds and do not touch unexploded bombs.

In the event of HOSTILE aircraft being seen in country districts, the nearest Naval, Military or Police Authorities should, if possible, be advised immediately by telephone of the TIME OF APPEARANCE, the DIRECTION OF FLIGHT, and whether the aircraft is an Airship or an Aeroplane.

GERMAN | **BRITISH**
AIRSHIPS | AIRSHIPS

AEROPLANES

AEROPLANES

This British poster advised people to learn to identify aircraft, so that they could shelter from the enemy.

During the war a large number of women in Europe exchanged their full-time jobs —for example in domestic service or in textile industries—for other kinds of work. Some undertook munitions production; others did farm work. Women were also needed as nurses and in back-up jobs to the armed forces. Many had to adapt quickly to being head of the household, although their status and rights were still not equal to those of men.

Land Girls

In Britain, the Women's Land Army was organized by the Board of Trade, rather than the War Office. WLA members, known as "land girls," did agricultural work. By the end of 1917, more than 250,000 women were working on British farms. They did the work of men who were away fighting and helped greatly with food supply.

A young Land Army woman cuts hay.

The Zeppelin's crew of 20 were carried in a gondola beneath the airship.

L 32

Air Raids

Gas-filled Zeppelin airships (named after German designer Count Ferdinand von Zeppelin) made their first bombing raids in 1914, on the Belgian city of Liège. The rigid airships could fly high and for long distances. The following year they started attacking Paris and London, striking fear into the hearts of many civilians. During 31 raids on London, 670 people were killed. Altogether the Germans used 115 Zeppelins during the war.

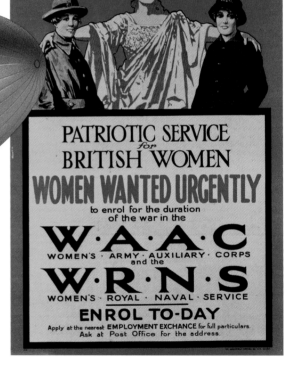

PATRIOTIC SERVICE *for* **BRITISH WOMEN**

WOMEN WANTED URGENTLY

to enrol for the duration of the war in the

W·A·A·C
WOMEN'S · ARMY · AUXILIARY · CORPS
and the

W·R·N·S
WOMEN'S · ROYAL · NAVAL · SERVICE

ENROL TO-DAY

Apply at the nearest EMPLOYMENT EXCHANGE for full particulars.
Ask at Post Office for the address.

British women were encouraged to enrol for "patriotic service." The WAAC was founded in 1917 and numbered 57,000 by 1918.

Nursing the Wounded

Professional nurses were joined by volunteers in military hospitals at home and in the field. The male-dominated authorities that were against women's involvement in the war were happy for them to help the wounded. In field hospitals, women were exposed to horror and danger. Many served far from home; Australian nurses, for example, worked as far afield as France, Egypt, and India.

English nurse Edith Cavell, who was nursing in Belgium, was executed by the Germans in 1915 for helping Allied soldiers escape.

Female Recruits

In some countries women were enrolled into supporting military organizations. Members of the British Women's Army Auxiliary Corps wore khaki uniforms and worked as clerks, telephonists, and gas-mask instructors. Their female leaders were not commissioned as officers, but were called controllers and administrators. Private soldiers were "workers." Similar auxiliary groups formed in other countries, and in Russia they had a more military role.

Entertaining the Troops

Since it was very difficult for theatrical groups to travel anywhere near the battlefield, troops of all nationalities mostly had to put on their own amateur shows if they ever had the time or energy. One exception was the French "army theater." French troops built their own stages, and were rewarded with visits by professional entertainers, including the famous French actresses Jeanne Bartet and Sarah Bernhardt.

French soldiers on leave were entertained by dancing shows in Paris and other cities. Light-hearted amusements lifted morale.

WOMEN AND THE HOME FRONT

1914
In Britain, the Women's Volunteer Reserve is founded. The Women's Hospital Corps sets up a military hospital in Paris, and later in London. In the Ottoman Empire, women begin working in offices, hospitals and schools for the first time.

1915
The British government appeals for women to join a Register of Women for War Service.

1916
American author Edith Wharton is made a French Chevalier of the Legion of Honor for her work with war refugees. In Britain, the Women's Royal Naval Service recruits cooks, clerks and wireless telegraphers (numbering 5,450 by 1918).

1917
Women play a leading role in the February Revolution (it took place in March according to the revised calendar of 1918) in Russia; a Russian women's battalion is founded.

1918
In the Ottoman Empire a female labor battalion is established. In Britain, both meat and sugar are rationed.

Women wartime workers in a German munitions factory.

Making Munitions

Women in all countries were needed as factory workers. In munitions factories, the work was hard and dangerous, since the materials for making weapons were poisonous and flammable. Though female workers were essential, they were still paid less than men. Most of the work was voluntary, but in Germany some women were forced into employment to help the war effort. Around 700,000 women worked in German munitions factories, and there were even more in Britain.

A German U-boat (from Unterseeboot, or submarine). Its main weapons were torpedoes with explosive warheads.

MAJOR OFFENSIVES

Major Offensives

On the Western Front, attacks by both sides generally ended in stalemate. This deadlocked trench warfare involved a huge loss of life. There were also enormous casualties on the Eastern Front, where the Germans and Austro-Hungarians attacked in 1915 and pushed the Russians back. At sea, German attacks on merchant ships helped persuade the United States to join the Allies, making a crucial difference to the balance of power.

Second Battle of Ypres

In late April 1915, the German Fourth Army began attacking Allied positions around the town of Ypres, on the Western Front in Flanders. The attack included the first large-scale use of poison gas (see page 35), which led to the Germans making ground against British, French and Canadian troops. They were unable to take Ypres itself, however, and so used heavy artillery to demolish it. The Allies lost almost 70,000 men – twice as many as the Germans.

This painting of the Second Battle of Ypres shows the chaos and horror of war.

War at Sea

In 1915 Germany began a submarine blockade of the British Isles, attacking merchant ships bringing supplies across the Atlantic. The sinking of the *Lusitania*, a passenger ship on the way from New York to Liverpool, caused outrage in Britain and anti-German feeling in the United States. British and German warships had their one direct encounter in the following year, at the Battle of Jutland.

I WANT YOU
FOR U.S. ARMY
NEAREST RECRUITING STATION

During the First World War, America produced thousands of recruitment posters encouraging people to sign up.

Verdun

The 10-month-long Battle of Verdun, in 1916, was the longest of the war. It was launched by the Germans in order to try and knock the French army out of the war. The German army was led by Crown Prince Wilhelm, eldest son of the Kaiser, and the French by Philippe Pétain, who famously promised, "They shall not pass." At the end of the offensive, Germany had gained a few miles along the Western Front. Figures for those killed and wounded are uncertain, but are in the region of several hundred thousand for both sides.

French soldiers in damaged Verdun, 1916.

Battle of the Somme

In July 1916 in France, British troops attacked north of the River Somme and French troops attacked south of the river. On the very first day, the British suffered 58,000 casualties, a third of them killed. General Douglas Haig led more attacks, supported by the French, but the Germans brought in reinforcements and little success was achieved. Terrible losses drained the manpower resources of both sides. The battle cost about 620,000 British and French and 500,000 German lives, and the Allies ended up gaining about 7.5 miles (12 km) of battle-scarred ground.

Soldiers on the Somme battlefields often had to fight, eat, sleep, and die in the thick mud, which penetrated everything. This horse-drawn unit is struggling to transport ammunition in the appalling conditions.

War diary entries, like this British Intelligence report made on the first day of the Somme offensive, provide information on troop movements.

Nivelle Offensive

France's General Nivelle planned a 1917 spring offensive near the River Aisne, aiming to smash through the German lines quickly. Some other military leaders opposed the operation, and when it failed, the French army was crippled and Nivelle was dismissed. There was mutiny among French soldiers, who had lost faith in their commanders and could see little point in more bloodshed. Pétain restored order, but the British had to take over the offensive role in France.

General Robert Nivelle (1856–1924) became commander-in-chief of French forces in December 1916. He was replaced by Marshal Pétain four months later.

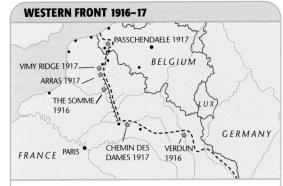

WESTERN FRONT 1916–17

PASSCHENDAELE 1917

VIMY RIDGE 1917

ARRAS 1917

THE SOMME 1916

BELGIUM

LUX

GERMANY

FRANCE   PARIS

CHEMIN DES DAMES 1917

VERDUN 1916

Attacks Made Minor Gains

In 1916, the main attack from the Germans was at Verdun. The Allies' major offensive was along the Somme, which was partly a counterattack to try and draw German troops away from Verdun. Long, hard-fought battles with enormous casualties led to very small changes in the location of the Front. In early 1917, the Germans withdrew behind the Hindenburg Line.

- - - - Front line in 1917
⊓⊔ Hindenberg line
✴ Major battles

Armistice and Afterwards

The poppy became a symbol to commemorate those who died in the war.

After failed German offensives early in 1918 and a defeat in northern France in the summer, the Kaiser installed a new government in Berlin. Many German politicians wanted to seek a peace agreement, but before they could do so, mutiny broke out in the navy and revolution among workers. In November, Wilhelm II was forced to abdicate, Germany became a republic and its representatives signed an armistice. The war was over.

Spring Offensives

In spring 1918, the Germans used reinforcements from the east to make five major attacks on the Western Front. Their aim was to win the war in France before any build-up of US forces. The attacks made early gains, but both sides suffered heavy losses. The final advance was turned back near the River Marne, just 50 miles (80 km) from Paris.

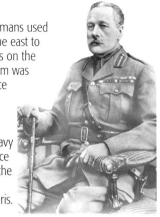

Field Marshal Sir Douglas Haig (1861–1928) commanded the British Expeditionary Force. Some of his tactics were criticized by Prime Minister David Lloyd George.

German Problems

Towards the end of the war there were severe food shortages in Germany. Bread had been rationed since 1915, and other foods were scarce. The situation was made worse by raging inflation. In 1918 a loaf of bread cost a quarter of a Mark; by 1922 it cost 3.50 Marks, and the following year rose to 100,000 Marks!

Inflation meant that after the war German banknotes became almost worthless.

The Kaiser Abdicates

By autumn 1918, Germany was near collapse. Its people lost faith in their leaders and there were riots. In early October power was transferred to parliament and the imperial chancellor announced the abdication of Wilhelm II on November 9. The Army helped its former emperor flee to the neutral Netherlands, where he officially gave up his throne. Wilhelm stayed there for the rest of his life.

The Royal Palace in Berlin was the Kaiser's main residence. After his abdication, it became a museum.

Fourteen Points

In January 1918, US President Woodrow Wilson named Fourteen Points as a proposal for a peace settlement. They included proposals for free trade and independence for Turkey and Poland. The final point called for an association of nations to help keep world peace. The proposals formed a basis for later discussions, but other Allied nations felt that they were not tough enough on Germany.

President Wilson's proposals for a peace settlement were widely publicized.

Program for the Peace of the World
By PRESIDENT WILSON, January 8, 1918

Armistice

Immediately after the Kaiser abdicated, German politicians met the Allied supreme commander in the forest of Compiègne, near Paris. They signed an armistice, and the ceasefire came into effect at 11 a.m. on 11 November, 1918 (at the 11th hour of the 11th day of the 11th month). Germany surrendered its arms and had to leave its occupied territories within 14 days. The following year, Allied countries declared 11th November to be Armistice Day, to commemorate those killed in the war.

Survivors

In addition to the 10 million soldiers killed, around nine million civilians died as a result of the war. Those who survived suffered severe hardship. Towns, villages and farmland were ruined, especially in northern France and Belgium. Many wounded soldiers came back to their families to discover that they had to find new homes.

Refugees left their homes to flee the fighting. Many returned to find destruction.

A London newspaper announces the armistice.

GERMAN TERRITORIAL LOSSES

Lost Territory
Defeat led to Germany giving up territory to Belgium, Denmark, France and Poland. Germany also lost its overseas colonies. France gained control of the Saar coalfields, and Saarland was controlled by the League of Nations. Allied troops occupied the Rhineland.

- ■ Lost
- ■ Occupied by Allied troops
- □ Saar

Map labels: DENMARK, HOLLAND, BELGIUM, FRANCE, SWITZERLAND, GERMANY, EAST PRUSSIA, WEST PRUSSIA, POLAND, CZECH REPUBLIC, AUSTRIA

ARMISTICE AND AFTERWARDS

1918
Mar 3
The Central Powers and Russia sign a peace agreement (Treaty of Brest-Litovsk).

Mar 21
Germans open their Spring Offensive (also called Kaiserschlacht or Second Battle of the Somme).

Apr 9
Second Spring Offensive begins along the River Lys.

Apr 14
Marshal Ferdinand Foch of France becomes Allied Supreme Commander on the Western Front.

May 27
Third Spring Offensive begins near the River Aisne (Third Battle of the Aisne).

Sep 29
Bulgaria surrenders.

Oct 4
The German government asks for a ceasefire.

Oct 30
The Ottoman Empire makes peace.

Nov 3
Austria-Hungary makes peace.

Nov 4
English war poet Wilfred Owen is killed in action in France.

Nov 9
Germany is proclaimed a republic.

Nov 11
Germany signs an armistice; official date of the end of the Great War.

Canadians celebrate Armistice Day. More than 56,000 Canadian soldiers were killed in the Great War.

The Russian Revolution

At the beginning of the 20th century, the vast Russian Empire was ruled by a tsar (or emperor) and a small group of wealthy aristocrats. Most Russians were poor peasants farming the land, though industrialization had taken many to work in the growing cities. Political revolutionaries wanted to change the system and bring better living conditions to the majority. As they gained support, there was a series of revolutions that led to Russia becoming a communist republic.

People supported the revolution because they wanted to end poverty and injustice. The Bolsheviks promised "peace, land, and bread."

Bloody Sunday

On January 22, 1905, 200,000 unarmed workers marched to the tsar's Winter Palace in St. Petersburg. The workers wanted reforms, but the imperial troops opened fire on the marchers and many were killed. This became known as the Bloody Sunday massacre, and it sparked a revolutionary reaction. By October there was a general strike, which forced the tsar to introduce an elected parliament (the Duma) with the power to pass laws. However, the tsar and his officials continued to interfere with the Duma.

The terrible events of Bloody Sunday were portrayed by Russian artist Vladimir Makovsky in his painting Death in the Snow.

Poverty and Discontent

Under the tsar, peasants worked hard to farm land rented from rich landowners. They struggled to make ends meet and were often in debt because of high rents and taxes. Some of their money helped to pay for new factories and railways, as industry grew in Russia, but this was of little benefit to the poor. The gap between wealthy aristocrats and pitifully poor workers led to growing discontent.

Peasant children often had to go hungry. Their parents were desperate for a better life.

Conflict with Japan

The Russo-Japanese War of 1904–05 ended in a humiliating defeat for the Russians (see page 24). The final land battle in China left the Russian army with 89,000 casualties, and was followed by the Russian Baltic Fleet being destroyed at sea. Defeat left a desperate situation, with mutiny in the army, riots in the streets and food shortages everywhere.

In this illustration from a 1904 journal, a correspondent films the Russian cavalry in Manchuria (northeast China).

Statue of the revolutionary leader Lenin (1870–1924), whose real name was Vladimir Ilyich Ulyanov.

Bolshevik Revolution

In October 1917, revolutionary Bolsheviks led workers and soldiers to the Winter Palace, the former royal residence in Petrograd (formerly St Petersburg) that had become government headquarters. The Bolsheviks formed a new government headed by Lenin. His new regime promised great changes, including an end to Russia's involvement in the Great War.

Armband of a Red Guard supporting the Bolsheviks.

The Tsar is Executed

After the Duma called on the tsar to abdicate, Nicholas II gave up the throne on March 15, 1917. The provisional government imprisoned Nicholas and his family, and they were moved several times. When it seemed possible that they might be rescued by anti-Bolshevik forces the following year, all the family were taken into a cellar and shot.

Right: Tsar Nicholas II (1868–1918) was the last Romanov ruler of Russia.

THE RUSSIAN REVOLUTION

1903
The Russian Social Democratic Workers' Party splits into Bolsheviks (the "majority," led by Lenin) and Mensheviks ("minority").

1905
Striking workers form the Soviet (or Council) of Workers' Deputies to coordinate revolutionary activities; Leon Trotsky is elected president of the St. Petersburg soviet.

1914
Russia joins the Allies in the First World War as part of the Triple Entente with Britain and France.

1916
Murder of Rasputin, a priest who had great influence over the tsar's wife as a supposed prophet and healer.

1917
February Revolution (took place in March according to the revised calendar of 1918) leads to provisional government and abdication of the tsar; October or Bolshevik Revolution (November in the new calendar) leads to a new government headed by Lenin.

1918
Russia signs a truce with Germany and loses territory. The Bolsheviks change their name to the Russian Communist Party.

Picasso's Violin and Guitar *(1912) combines the shapes of the two instruments.*

Pablo Picasso (1881–1973) moved to France in 1904.

Cubism

The art movement known as Cubism revolutionized European painting and sculpture. The movement began in France about 1907 and flourished until 1914. The leaders of Cubism were the Spanish-born artist Pablo Picasso and French artist Georges Braque. They used geometric (or "cubic") shapes to represent solid forms in two dimensions, often using many different views of an object in a single image.

Chagall's Birthday *(1915) is typical of his fanciful style. The man in the picture floats upside down and contorts his body.*

Musical Trends

French composer Claude Debussy (1862–1918) introduced a new musical approach known as impressionism. Some of his works include sounds that give the impression of wind or the sea. The works of Austrian composer Arnold Schoenberg (1874–1951) and Russian-born Igor Stravinsky (1882–1971) were more revolutionary and experimental. They used unusual rhythms and conflicting sounds that were not always popular at the time.

The young Stravinsky. He wrote famous ballet scores, such as The Firebird *(1910) and* The Rite of Spring *(1913).*

Picasso's Violin and Guitar *(1912) combines the shapes of the two instruments.*

Dreamlike Fantasy

Artists such as Russian-born Marc Chagall (1887–1985), who went to Paris in 1910, combined elements of fantasy and dreams. Chagall was greatly influenced by Cubism. Many of the figures and animals in his pictures float through the air, and art historians consider that his style influenced the 1920s movement of Surrealism.

The Arts

There were many new movements in the early 1900s. European and North American painters, writers and musical composers were looking for new directions. They moved away from traditional 19th-century approaches and became more experimental. Painters, for example, turned from realistic representation to more abstract styles. Later in the period these movements were influenced by the First World War, which brought great social and political upheaval. The war also left many artists feeling bitter and pessimistic, which may be reflected in their work.

Questioning Art

Revolutionary artists such as French-born Marcel Duchamp (1887–1968) posed the question, "What is art?" In 1913, Duchamp produced his first "ready-made," which was simply an ordinary bicycle wheel. Two years later, he went to the United States, where he was already well known for his unconventional paintings. Many people said his works were meaningless, or even disgraceful, but they certainly invited gallery-goers to look at everyday objects in a new way.

Duchamp sent this urinal, entitled Fountain, *to the first exhibition of the Society of Independent Artists, in 1917.*

Art Nouveau

The decorative style of "new art," named after a Paris art gallery, flourished from about 1890 to 1910. It was used a great deal in graphic design, for books and posters, as well as for jewellery, glassware and ornamental objects. Many of its works incorporated the shapes of flowers and plants. The style became known by many different names, including Jugendstil in Germany, Sezessionstil in Austria and Stile Floreale in Italy. In the United States, the designer Louis Comfort Tiffany (1848–1933) created colorful glassware in the art nouveau style.

This elaborate candlestick from 1900 is designed in the Art Nouveau style. It takes the form of a woman entwined with thistle-shaped flowers.

Viennese Culture

Turn-of-the-century Vienna, capital of Austria-Hungary, was a flourishing cultural centre. The pioneering psychiatrist Sigmund Freud (1856–1939) established an International Psychoanalytical Society there. Freud's new ideas influenced many Viennese writers and artists, including playwright and novelist Arthur Schnitzler (1862–1931) and painter Gustav Klimt (1862–1918). Gustav Mahler and his fellow composer Schoenberg were also working there at this time.

Fulfilment (1905–09) by Gustav Klimt, who founded an avant-garde group called the Sezession in Vienna.

Sigmund Freud developed new theories about the symbolism of dreams.

Glossary

Anarchist Somebody who rejects the need for a system of government, authority or control in society, and favors political disorder.

Aristocracy People of noble birth or the highest social class; also called gentry or High Society.

Aviation Operating and flying aircraft.

Aviatrix A female aviator (pilot).

Back projection The projection of a still or moving picture on to the back of a screen for use as a background when filming.

Bakelite A trademarked synthetic resin (or early plastic), used mainly for electrical equipment. It was named after its inventor, L.H.Baekeland.

Balkans The mountainous peninsula region of southeastern Europe between the Adriatic and Ionian Seas in the west and the Aegean and Black Seas in the east. Historically, the Balkan countries have included Albania, Bosnia and Herzegovina, Bulgaria, Croatia, Greece, Macedonia, Montenegro, Romania, Serbia, Slovenia, part of Turkey, and Yugoslavia.

Battalion A large military unit, especially of infantry, ready for battle.

British Expeditionary Force An army created by reforms in 1908 and sent to France in 1914.

Bureaucrats Government officials, especially those who apply rules rigidly.

Cave of the Thousand Buddhas A 7th-century Buddhist cave temple on the banks of the Yishui River in eastern China, discovered by westerners in 1907.

Christian missionaries Church men and women who have traveled to a foreign country to teach the Christian faith and convert the people there to Christianity.

Colony An area that is ruled by another country and occupied by settlers (colonials).

Communist A supporter of a classless society in which all property is owned by the community of people and everyone contributes and receives according to their abilities and needs. The Communist state controls the economy.

Conscription Compulsory enrolment into the armed forces.

Conservative Relating to the British Conservative Party, which grew out of the Tories in the 1830s and promotes free enterprise and private ownership.

Dada movement A movement in art, literature, music and film that mocked artistic conventions and stressed the illogical and absurd.

Democracy A system of government representing all its citizens equally through elected representatives and based on majority decision-making.

Diphtheria A serious, contagious bacterial disease that affects breathing and damages the heart and nervous system.

Dual Monarchy Two autonomous states governed by a common sovereign. The Dual Monarchy of Austria-Hungary (also known as the Austro-Hungarian Empire) was ruled by the Habsburgs from 1867 to 1918.

Emancipation Setting free from social restrictions; liberation, especially the improvement of women's rights.

Empire style A style of dress (as well as furniture and decoration) influenced by classical designs. The name refers back to the First Empire in France (1804–15).

Equality League of Self-Supporting Women An American women's suffrage group, formed in 1907, which included working-class women and held parades and open-air meetings.

Fabian Society An organization founded in London in 1884 to promote gradual (rather than revolutionary) socialist reform.

Great Naval Review A ceremonial presentation of the huge British naval fleet at Spithead, in the English Channel, in 1909.

Guerrilla tactics A kind of warfare carried out by small irregular (unofficial) units, usually against a larger regular army and with political aims against a government.

Irish Republican Brotherhood An Irish-American revolutionary nationalist organization founded in 1858. Members were called Fenians.

Labour Party A political party formed in the UK in 1906 (from the Labour Representative Committee) to represent the interests of ordinary working people.

Law Code of Hammurabi A collection of laws made by the ancient Babylonian ruler Hammurabi (reigned 1792–1750 BCE).

Liberal government The administration of the Liberal Party, one of the two major British political parties in the early 1900s. It emerged from the old Whig Party in the 1860s. The Liberals brought in social welfare legislation.

Mesopotamia The region of Southwest Asia between the Tigris and Euphrates rivers (in present-day Iraq).

Mobilize To prepare and organize troops for active service.

Multiple-reel films Long films that are divided into several parts for projection.

Munitions Military ammunition, weapons, equipment and stores.

Nationalists People with strong patriotic feelings who want political independence for their country.

Offensive A military attack.

Orphism An abstract form of the Cubism art movement that emphasized harmony of color.

Qing Dynasty A series of rulers established by the Manchus that ruled China from 1644 to 1912, ending with the last emperor of China.

Republic A state in which people elect representatives to exercise power. A republic is headed by an elected or nominated president, instead of a monarch.

Sezession An avant-garde group of German and Austrian artists who organized their own independent exhibitions.

Slavs A group of peoples in central and Eastern Europe who speak Slavic languages (such as Bulgarian, Polish or Russian).

Socialists Those supporting the political system by which the means of production and distribution are owned and controlled by the community as a whole.

Stop motion A film technique in which the camera is repeatedly stopped and started to create the impression of movement.

Surrealism An avant-garde movement in art and literature that represented the unconscious mind with fantastic and contradictory images. The works have an element of surprise.

Women's Social and Political Union A British movement, founded in 1903 by Emmeline and Christabel Pankhurst, that staged public demonstrations and campaigned for women to be able to vote. It was the first group whose members were known as "suffragettes."

Workhouse An institution in which the poor were given food and accommodation in return for unpaid work.

Index